The Songs *in* My Heart

Seasonal Remembrances

ANNE MARIE GINNANE

ISBN 979-8-89043-658-0 (paperback)
ISBN 979-8-89043-659-7 (digital)

Christian Faith Publishing
832 Park Avenue
Meadville, PA 16335
www.christianfaithpublishing.com

Printed in the United States of America

To family and friends

Spring

Sunshine
Big white puffy clouds
Cries of early morning birds overhead
Fresh air
Babbling brook
Snapping twigs
Freshly pruned bushes
Heavy flower scent
Creaking shed door
Fresh house paint
Laughter of children
Smack of jumping rope hitting pavement
Hope of spring begets new life.

The Morning

Sun peeking through curtains
Early morning rush
Muffled sounds
Coffee brewing
Toaster popping
Eggs sizzling in a pan
Newspaper rattling
Faucet water dripping
Feet running
Doors slamming
School bus horn honking
Car radio blaring
Suddenly quiet, very quiet, for the day has begun.

The Kitchen Table

Scarred wooden furniture
Flutter of red gingham curtains
Shine of toaster
Click of oven door
Blue cereal bowl filled
Bacon sizzling and snapping
Coffee cake crumbs scattered on table
Steaming coffee cup
Orange juice in a flowered glass
Frayed cloth napkin
Hum of refrigerator
Dishes rattling in sink
Day beginning, a promising start.

The Backyard

Painted azure blue sky
Curtains ruffling at window.
Wooden basket of wet clothes
Sheets flapping in breeze
Fence door creaking
Green grass dotted with dandelions
Broken flowers
Sizzle of neighbor's barbecue
Children calling to one another
Swings creaking
Crack of ball hitting bat
Stuffed animal half-buried in dirt
A fresh start to a long week.

The Apple Tree

In spring, green buds bloom
Fluffy blossoms fill the air
Delicate scents
Insects hum
Butterflies perch
Birds build nests
In autumn, smell of ripe fruit
Plop of apples on the ground
Leaves scattered across hardened ground
Trees black and wet in rain
Naked stiff branches scrape ground
Tree decorated with jewel-like icicles
Autumn finish leads to a winter farewell and spring birth.

Easter

Slight breeze
Colorful tulips swaying
Car doors slamming
Footsteps on church steps
Smell of furniture polish
Scratch of palms on pews
Voices calling out in greeting
Crinkle of new Easter bonnets
Easter hymns sung
Clatter of the Easter feast
Crinkle of candy foil
Jellybeans dropped in bowl
Celebration at dawn for He has risen.

Summer

Bright sun
Patchwork fields of green and yellow
Rush of wind through tall grass
Splash of summer shower on windows
Birds chirping
Frogs croaking
Waft of flowers
Shovel hitting dirt
Low hum of lawnmower
Slap of flesh on the slide
Creak of a swing set in the breeze
Kites floating in the sky
Summer beckons with a warm welcome.

The Countryside

Birds overhead in formation
Windswept hills
Water dribbling over flat smooth rocks
Patches of wildflowers
Smell of fresh grass
Splintering of the old wooden fence
Grinding of tree stumps
Rumble of tractor engine
Freshly plowed earth
Smell of cut hay
Cows mooing
Cantor of horses
A place of refuge and rest to tend the soul.

The Front Porch

Sun setting on horizon
Creak of rocking chair
Drone of bees in bushes
Hum of lawnmower
Footsteps on old wooden steps
Sound of squeaky stair board
Slap of thrown newspaper
Swish of broom
Clink of mailbox
Screen door opening and closing
Whine of radio
Teacup rattling
Day is done. All is good.

The Neighbor's Homestead

Sentinel trees standing guard
Drip of water from eaves
Broken windows heaving
Shutters banging against house
Tattered quilt airing
Clang of old car rotting
Rusted metal shed banging
Ripped scarecrow waving
Birds scratching bare dirt
Crunch of dried leaves
Glimpse of broken trail
Muddy boot prints leading into woods
A sense of an incomplete, unfinished existence.

The Picnic

Gentle breeze
Whoosh of weeping willow tree
Crunch of footsteps on gravel
Basket unfastened
Picnic table groaning
Crinkle of foil
Slap of paper plates
Smell of fried chicken
Coffee aroma escaping from thermos
Children romping
Seesaw creaking
Swings squeaking
A lazy day, a fruitful and happy day.

The Dock on the Lake

Sun beating down
Mass of trees surrounded by bushes
Echo of wind in the trees
Old weather-beaten dock
Murky green water swirling
Rhythmic waves hitting dock
Rowboat banging against dockside
Sound of running feet on broken planks
Cries of laughter
Fishing poles scattered
Small boats hovering in distance
Sun setting on horizon
Day is done and with it, the promise of tomorrow.

The Sunset

Local waterfront activities
Scavenger gulls screaming
Breeze oscillating
Sound of distant motorboats
Awnings flapping in the breeze
Fishermen squatting with poles
Murmured voices
Clatter of many pails
Knives cutting on wooden board
Fish grilling
Soft hum of pier lights
Sunsetting, a yellow-orange globe on horizon
Day's end. Another story, another journey completed.

Fall

Brisk autumn air
Lake shimmering in afternoon sun
Fresh smell of pinecones
Wood being piled
Odor of burning wood
Dried leaves being raked
Nestling by the campfire
Worn afghan covering rocker
Click of knitting needles
Tea kettle whistling
Homemade bread baking
Whiffs of hot spicy cider
Fall's deep quiet matches soulful depth and tranquility.

The Farmhouse

Blanketed by snow patches
Old bicycle leaning against steps
Scrape of shovel on pavement
Rusted gate creaking on hinges
Vegetable bins emptied
Faded curtains fluttering
Frayed rug crumpled on wood floor
Threadbare coat dangling from hook
Crumpled clothes in bin
Hairbrush on bureau
Faded pictures stuck on dresser mirror
Tunes from plastic jewelry box
Home, home at last.

The Church

Peal of bells in belfry
Light through stained glass windows
Flickering candles
Scent of altar flowers
Faint organ music playing
Choir voices singing hymns
Footsteps moving with soft rhythm
Rattle of beads on clerical flock
Closing of confessional door
Chairs scraping
Thump of prayer books
Low voices murmuring
Calmness and order, a peace that passes all understanding.

The School Day

Early morning bell
Windows opened
Bookbags thrown in closets
Greetings
Books hitting desks
Loud laughter
Rustle of papers
Whisperings
Chalk squeaking on blackboard
Feet shuffling on floor
Scratch of pencils on paper
Smell of wax crayons
Routine training that results in creativity and growth.

City Life

Wind moving in overhead trees
Thump of cars on road
Slam of taxi doors
Police whistles noted
Ambulance sirens screaming
Carriages driven by horses in the park
Pavements cracking
Vagrant sleeping on a bench
Shuffle of feet on subway stairs
Click-clack of high heels on sidewalk
Cries of doorman
Rolled newspapers hitting ground
A fast-paced lifestyle with endless possibilities.

The Circus

Big top with red and white stripes
Brightly colored awnings
Yellowed ticket stubs
Sideshow attractions
Bright, sparkly costumes
Deep voice of ringmaster
Show animals in the ring
Laughter of audience
Children howling with glee
Clowns dancing
Organ grinder with dancing monkey
Smell of cotton candy
A fantasy experience with a lifetime of memories.

The Cemetery

Sounds of late autumn
Cry of lone bird overhead
Afternoon sun cooling
Whisper of the trees
Long uneven shadows stretching
Leaves falling softly to the ground
Cacophony of faraway sounds
Weathered gate swinging
Car doors closing
Flowers placed at graves
Stone angel perched on tombstone
Voices uplifted in prayer
Silence of metaphysical light, energy, and sound.

Winter

Windswept plains covered with snow
Lacey snowflakes falling to the ground
Icicles, long streaming silver ornaments, hanging
Street lights flickering
Figures skating on the pond
Boots crunching
Clumps of ice cracking
Snow melting on mailbox
Animal tracks seen around the house
Sledding children shouting
Dogs barking
Red mitten buried in melting snow
Early flowering buds invite seasonal transition and spring birth.

The Grandfather Desk

Clock ticking on mantel
Civil War creation
Smooth lines visible
Wood richly polished
Curved handles broken
Claw feet carved
Crystal glass cantor shimmering in afternoon sun
Smell of peppermint and tobacco
Candlesticks gleaming on desktop
Phones ringing
Rumble of deep male voices
Stack of bills bundled
Reflections of a bygone, worthy era.

Christmas

Fire in fireplace snapping and crackling
Hiss of wood added to the fire
Pine scent of candles overpowering
Hum of Christmas tunes
Creak of old rocking chair
Tree twinkling with brightly colored lights
Shiny ornaments and baubles reflected
Hand-carved nativity scene glowing
Patter of little feet
Crinkle of wrapping paper
Ribbons cut and curled
Stockings hung from the mantel
Contemplation of the present embraces the whispers of memories past.

The Doll

Hidden under creaking floorboards
Covered with thin veil of dust
Facial features framed with delicate beauty
Body made of smooth plastic
Doll dress ripped
Faded pink material hand-sewn
Slipper missing
Hand chipped
Wig knotted
Hair ribbon tangled
Old locket rusting
Keeper of dreams and stories
For a child, the doll symbolizes future hope and unrealized aspirations.

First Kiss

Side glances across the room
Faint stirrings of interest
Smiles
Laughter
Discussions shared
Reaching, exploring
Sense of longing
Hand holding
Lips touching
Hearts beating
Lips locking
Farewell lingering
Start of romance and love.

First Date

Shy smiles
Furtive glances
Feet shuffling
Lingering looks
Menus opening
Napkins unfolding
Glasses filled
Dinner rushing
Murmured exchanges
Laughter
End of meal, chairs scraping
Veiled goodbyes
Date over. The beginning of courtship.

The Kaleidoscope of Life

Infancy to childhood
Start of schooling, end of schooling
Onset of spiritual journey
Development of friendships
Marriage and family initiated
Beginning of military service, end of military service
Career begins, career ends
Retirement planned
Health to infirmity
Recognition of life lessons
Old age to death
Spiritual journey ends
Passing of time measured in rich, varied mosaics.

About the Author

Now in her seventh decade of life, Anne Marie Ginnane has lived a long and productive life. Raised by a business couple along with two siblings, her training and life experiences have been in education, business, history, and the arts. The author also served in the army and is a military veteran.

Ms. Ginnane has visited and lived in several parts of the country, which enabled her to become acquainted with its many parts and incredible diversity. In addition, Anne Marie has always been a producer of creative thought and a writer of different forms. This book, a collection of assorted remembrances, came to her while in prayerful thanksgiving to God for becoming cancer free. Today, Ms. Ginnane has a new and exciting interest in her life: being a grandmother.

www.ingramcontent.com/pod-product-compliance
Lightning Source LLC
Chambersburg PA
CBHW020855160726
47993CB00004B/1667